DRAKE

An Unauthorized Biography

Table of Contents

Introduction

Aubrey Drake Graham, also known as Drizzy Drake, is a Canadian recording artist and actor. Hailing from Toronto, Ontario, Drake first launched his career playing Jimmy Brooks on the Canadian television teen drama series, *Degrassi: The Next Generation*. However, Drake's true love was music. After releasing several mixtapes via the internet, Drake finally hit it big as an independent artist, with his singles, "Best I Ever Had" and "Every Girl."

Drake was quickly scooped up by Young Money Entertainment and, as a result, had rapping sensation Lil Wayne as a hip hop mentor. His career has shown no signs of faltering. His recent single, "Take Care," featuring Rihanna, has been topping charts around the world.

Drake is in hot demand by the music industry. He has worked with international hip hop legends, such as Rick Ross, Kanye West, Eminem, Jay-Z, and Nicki Minaj.

Standing at six feet two inches, this first-ever black Jewish rap star has shown that hard work and dedication can take you anywhere. This unauthorized biography follows Drake's career from his early days as a teenage actor to his struggles as an independent music artist, and to finally becoming what he has always wanted: an internationally known hip hop artist.

Early Life

Drake: "I do put an immense amount of pressure on myself; I don't sleep much. I think about everything and everyone in my life and trying to make everyone happy. My best friend tells me that I care too much, that I want everyone to like me. Not everyone's gonna like you, but I just want to be remembered as a man that somebody wants to be."

Aubrey Drake Graham was born on October 24, 1986, in Toronto, Ontario, to parents Dennis and Sandi Graham. Dennis was a drummer who worked with Jerry Lee Lewis, and Sandi, who originally wished to name her son Abraham, was an educator. Drake's father is African-American and hails from Memphis, Tennessee. His mother is white and Jewish Canadian.

Drake's musical education began early. When he was a young child, his father would take him to late night club gigs in Toronto.

"I knew how to sing 'Ride, Sally, Ride,' which is a cover he'd perform, and he'd bring me up onstage with him to sing it as part of his act."

Drake's parents divorced when he was only five years old, and Drake went to live with his mother in Toronto's Forest Hill, an affluent, predominantly Jewish neighborhood. His parents' divorce had a profound effect on Drake:

"I had to become a man very quickly and be the backbone for a woman who I love with all of my heart, my mother."

Drake attended elementary school at Forest Hill Public School and high school at Forest Hill Collegiate Institute. Attending school in such a homogeneous area was tough for Drake; he felt that "nobody understood what it was like to be black and Jewish." It was in high school that Drake first tried his hand at acting.

> *"There was a kid in my class whose father was an agent. His dad would say, 'If there's anyone in the class that makes you laugh, have them audition for me.' After the audition, he became my agent."*

Musical ability undoubtedly runs in Drake's family. Aside from his father, two of Drake's uncles, Mabon "Teenie" Hodges and Larry Graham, were also musicians. Larry Graham was the bassist in Sly and the Family Stone and also played with Prince. Teenie Hodges was a guitarist who co-wrote "Take Me to the River" and "Love and Happiness" with Al Green. Drake comments on how important music was to his family while growing up:

> *"I grew up around classic, timeless music, like George Benson and the Spinners. My Jewish side of the family is very musical; my cousins are very skilled in piano and graduated from arts and music schools."*

When young Drake decided to pursue acting, his parents were very supportive and encouraging.

"My father and my mother are both people who definitely support anything in the arts. My father is a musician and my mother's side is immersed in music and acting."

Drake was raised Jewish by his mother and attended Jewish day school. His bar mitzvah in held the basement of an Italian restaurant in Toronto. Although he identifies with being an African-American, Drake still recognizes his Jewish background:

"At the end of the day, I consider myself a black man because I'm more immersed in black culture than any other. Being Jewish is kind of a cool twist. It makes me unique."

To this day, Drake claims that he still celebrates all of the Jewish holidays with his mother and maintains that someday he would like to travel to Israel. He remains very close to his mother.

"My mother made me truly appreciate women. I obviously make sex-driven, darker, sexier music, but I try not to offend women in them. It's not in my character. And my father was basically a reverse role model for me. I'm dying to be a great dad one day, whenever that day comes. Other than that, it was hard just growing up with my mom and watching her fight for me to have a good childhood. It was tough to watch."

Drake is so close with his mother that, in July 2010, he cancelled his entire European tour in order to be with his mother, who was scheduled for surgery. Drake confirmed that his mother had been battling an illness for a considerable length of time, but did not reveal what the specific ailment was.

Although he lived with his mother in Canada during the school year, summers were typically spent with Drake's father, in Memphis. His father was instrumental in young Drake learning to rap.

"My dad was in jail for two years and he shared a cell with this dude who didn't really have anyone to speak to. So, he used to share his phone time with this dude and at the time I was probably 16 or 17, this dude was like 20 or 22, and he would always rap to me over the phone—it was Poverty, that was his rap name. I started to get into it and I started to write my own s–t down. He would call me and we would just rap to each other. And, after my dad got out, I kept in touch with the dude and eventually I accepted the fact that I wanted to be in music."

Degrassi: The Next Generation

Drake: "Degrassi was never something I saw as potentially ruining [a music career]. It was a great TV show. It had a cult following."

Although Drake had been cast in one episode of *Blue Murder*, a Canadian crime drama television series, his acting career took off when, at the young age of fourteen, he was cast as Jimmy Brooks in *Degrassi: The Next Generation* (renamed *Degrassi* in its tenth season), a Canadian teen television drama series. Drake was a regular cast member in the first seven seasons (a total of 138 episodes), as well as the 2008 television movie, *Degrassi Spring Break Movie*. His character is also mentioned in the 2010 television movie, *Degrassi Takes Manhattan*.

His character, James "Jimmy" Brooks, is a high school basketball star who becomes physically disabled after being shot in the back by a classmate. Jimmy comes from a wealthy family and is often seen wearing expensive clothing. Jimmy is best friends with another Degrassi character, Gavin "Spinner" Mason, although the two frequently fight and argue. Drake became very close with Shane Kippel, the actor who portrayed Mason.

"Well, my best friend here [Shane Kippel]...I hope that he'll come to my wedding and be one of my best men standing there on the side, me and Shane Kippel. We just formed the greatest relationship, and when I see him, it may sound weird, but it makes my day better, lights up my day when he walks in and I know I have scenes with him. He's just one of my favorite people to see walk through the door. I take to him as a person, and I think he's really grown as an actor. I think he's become a very, very talented individual. We just have the best conversations, we have the best jokes. That's my dude. I really care about that dude a lot."

Drake's character, Jimmy, dates Ashley until she takes the drug ecstasy and cheats on Jimmy at a party. The two teens eventually resume dating; however it is short lived, as Ashley has changed and she realizes Jimmy is in love with her old persona.

In seasons three, four, and five, Jimmy dates Hazel. At this point, Jimmy realizes he has feelings for Ellie, another Degrassi character. It is here in the series that Jimmy is shot in the back by Rick, causing him to use a wheelchair throughout the rest of his tenure on the show. Characters Spinner and Jay tricked Rick into believing that Jimmy had pulled a prank on Rick, and so Rick shot Jimmy in retribution. A conscientious actor, Drake took steps to prepare for this change in his character:

"Initially, when I found that I was going to be shot and end up in a wheelchair, I spent time with a wonderful kid who was shot and paralyzed. We went places in public and I just wanted to see how people treat you when you're in a wheelchair, and how people treated me for being with somebody in a

wheelchair, just capture a natural feeling about the overall situation. Now, it's just sort of second nature. I don't really have to work that hard at transferring it to Jimmy, because I've been doing it so long that that switch happens."

As Drake's character, Jimmy, had been a basketball star before his injury, Jimmy's father encourages him to play wheelchair basketball. However, Jimmy discovers a love for art and pursues this interest instead. After graduating high school in season seven (a year later than originally planned, due to the time he took off due to his injury), Jimmy decides to pursue a career in music. Jimmy's love for music is something that Drake shared with his character:

"Music is probably my first love. I mean, I love acting, I'll never give it up, but music is definitely something I put my heart into. When they wanted me to do music on the show, at first I was a little hesitant because I have a career as Drake, and I

wanted to keep it separate. I had a conversation with my agent and just a couple people I work with on music. It turned out great. I was actually listening to the song the other day, and I was like, wow, this isn't half bad for a song on a TV show. Yeah, the music thing is definitely a big, big deal for me."

Also in season seven, Jimmy starts to date Trina, another physically challenged individual. This would be the last season in which Jimmy was a regular character on *Degrassi: The Next Generation*. After the season ended in 2009, the producers cut many of the original characters and replaced them with fresh actors, an experience Drake found frustrating:

"We basically all came to work one day and we were all kind of fired in our own way. It was devastating for a lot of us. Our names were changed on our dressing rooms and we were like, 'What's happening?'"

The original *Degrassi* universe was created by Linda Schuyler and Kit Hood in 1979. The television series included in the *Degrassi* franchise include, in chronological order, *The Kids of Degrassi Street, Degrassi Junior High, Degrassi High,* and *Degrassi: The Next Generation.* Similar to the other series, *Degrassi: The Next Generation* follows a cast of students at the Degrassi Community School. The characters face various real-world teenage challenges, such as low self-esteem, peer pressure, drugs, abuse, sexuality, gang violence, teen pregnancy, death, and self-injury.

Degrassi: The Next Generation was created by Linda Schuyler and Yan Moore. It is produced by Epitome Pictures in association with CTV, a Canadian television network. Schuyler, along with her husband, Stephen Stohn, and Brendon Yorke are executive producers of the series. Filming takes place at Epitome's studios in Toronto, Ontario, Canada. The franchise is named after the real De Grassi Street in the same city.

When *Degrassi: The Next Generation* first aired, it was frequently cited as the most watched domestic drama series in Canada, as well as one of the highest-rated shows on the TeenNick network in the United States. Viewership was often cited at one million viewers per episode in Canada and just under half a million viewers in the United States.

Although the target audience age for *Degrassi: The Next Generation* is thirteen to seventeen, approximately forty percent of fans are outside of this demographic and are in their twenties and thirties. These fans were dedicated viewers of the earlier *Degrassi* series and enjoy the new addition to the franchise.

Critics praised *Degrassi: The Next Generation*, and the series received favorable reviews from *Entertainment Weekly* and *The New York Times*. The series has won over fifty awards from the Geminis, the Writers Guild of Canada, the Directors Guild of Canada, the Teen Choice Awards, the Young Artist Awards, Prix Jeunesse, and others. The series even has famous fans, such as filmmakers and actors Kevin Smith and Jason Mewes, who have both guest-starred on various episodes.

Although *Degrassi: The Next Generation* had successful beginnings, in recent years viewership has waned. Unfortunately, the number of viewers per episode has been declining since season six. In 2010, in season nine, the series was moved to CTV's MuchMusic, a youth-oriented channel. In an attempt to revitalize the series, the production style was changed in season ten. *Degrassi: The Next Generation* became a telenovela, a daily soap opera. Season eleven aired beginning on July 18, 2011, and a twelfth season has been ordered by MuchMusic.

Music Career

Drake: "I was planning on this being something worth mentioning, energy invested in someone I saw potential in."

Independent Career (2006–2009)

In February 2006, Drake launched his independent music career and released his first mixtape, *Room for Improvement*. The mixtape was originally intended for sale, but only sold six thousand copies in 2006. It was made available for free on his official website as well as his official MySpace page. *Room for Improvement* was re-released in 2009, featuring eleven selected songs as well as a remix of the track, "Do What You Do." In an early 2006 interview, Drake commented on his first mixtape:

"It's a mix CD and I did it with DJ Smallz who does the Southern Smoke Series. He's done mix tapes with everyone, Lil Wayne, Young Jeezy, a lot of people and he's hosting it for me. It's called Room For Improvement. Its seventeen original tracks and a couple of remixes and stuff like that. Twenty-two tracks in total. I have the Clipse on there, I got Trey Songz in there, I got Lupe Fiasco on there, I have Nickelus F, who is this amazing artist from Virginia who I'm very, very tight with and we work together a lot, we worked together. I have Voyce on there; he's a singer from Toronto. Production-wise, I don't really have any major producers on there. I have a song I did with Trey Songz. I have an individual by the name of Nick Rashur from Harlem — he's a really cool cat. Amir; Boi-1da did the majority of the singles... Who else should I mention? DJ Ra from DC, a lot of people on the CD."

Drake released a second mixtape, *Comeback Season*, in 2007. This mixtape spawned a single as well as a music video for the track, "Replacement Girl," which features rapper/producer/actor/songwriter Trey Songz. Terral "T.Slack" Slack of BPE Booking Company was the executive producer of the video.

With the "Replacement Girl" video, Drake became the first unsigned Canadian rapper to have a music video featured on Black Entertainment Television (BET). This honor was bestowed just as "Replacement Girl" was featured as the "New Joint of the Day" on April 30, 2007. Also featured on *Comeback Season* was a freestyle over a song with Lil Wayne, a remix of the track, "Man of the Year," which was originally performed by Brisco and Flo Rida.

In 2008, Rap-A-Lot founder Jas Prince (J. Prince's son) played Drake's early music for mogul Lil Wayne, who was impressed and immediately phoned Drake and invited him to fly to Houston, Texas, to tour with him. Lil Wayne was from Hollygrove, a destitute New Orleans neighborhood. It was immediately clear to Drake that the two of them were from different worlds:

"He was high out of his mind, getting these big wings tattooed on his body on the tour bus, for, like, six straight hours. And out of nowhere, everyone got on the bus and the bus started moving. I just kept my mouth shut. Rolled for like a week, ended up in Atlanta. That was the night we made our first bit of music together."

While on tour together, Drake and Lil Wayne recorded several songs together, including "Ransom," which was the original version of "I Want This Forever," and the remix of Drake's song, "Brand New." Although Drake was now officially a part of Lil Wayne's Young Money Crew, Drake was not signed to the Young Money Entertainment recording label.

After the release of his first two mixtapes, Drake was concerned that he might not make it as a music star:

"[I was] teetering on getting a regular job. I was coming to terms with the fact that, okay, people know me from Degrassi, but I might have to work at a restaurant or something just to keep things going. The money from that show was very small. And it was dwindling."

On February 13, 2009, Drake released his third independent mixtape, *So Far Gone.* Guest appearances included Lil Wayne, Bun B, Omariod, Lloyd, and Drake's close friend, Trey Songz.

Like his previous mixtapes, *So Far Gone* was offered as a free download on his official website. Within two hours of being released, the mixtape had been downloaded over two thousand times. *So Far Gone* continued to be extremely popular and eventually made its way to radio airwaves. MTV cited *So Far Gone* as "The Hottest Mixtape of 2009 (So Far)."

Two singles were released from *So Far Gone*: "Best I Ever Had" and "Successful." These two singles were immensely popular and, as a result, the mixtape was released as an EP on

September 15, 2009, featuring only five songs from the original mixtape as well as two new songs. The EP debuted at No. 6 on the *Billbaord 200*. The album has since been certified gold and has sold over half a million copies in the United States. The EP won Rap Recording of the Year at the 2010 Juno Awards, an award show for Canadian music artists.

Drake received a large amount of recognition for *So Far Gone,* and was nominated for several awards, including several Grammys, including "Best Rap Song" and "Best Rap Solo Performance" for the song, "Best I Ever Had."

On May 28, 2009, an unauthorized Drake album entitled *The Girls Love Drake* was released on iTunes, Rhapsody, and Amazon. The album was released by the Canadian Money Entertainment label and distributed by the Independent Online Distribution Alliance (IODA). The album featured songs from *So Far Gone*, as well as several new tracks.

Drake's management sent a letter to cease and desist, and the album was then pulled from all retail outlets. Drake's manager, Al Branch, commented on the scandal:

> *"This is a straight bootleg, a scandal. We are behind promoting records at radio, but haven't sold it. iTunes' position is that they are a store and they stock everything. They have a waiver and as long as people sign it and are responsible for the product they submit, then they go for it."*

Peter Greenwood, the founder of Canadian Money Entertainment, defended his actions by saying that his company has been releasing mixtapes for unsigned artists since 2003 and their intentions were not malevolent:

> *"'The Girls Love Drake' was just a combination of new and old songs that we had been promoting on the underground scene for the last six months and so we wanted to get more exposure for it on the net.*

Breaking him in the states along with other Toronto artists has always been our goal. Drake is our hometown hero."

So Far Gone continued to be surrounded by controversy and scandal. Kia Shine, an American rapper and producer, claimed that he had actually produced and co-wrote the track, "Best I Ever Had." Shine had previously produced a mixtape track for Lil Wayne titled, "Do It For The Boy," in which the phrase, "best I ever had" is a lyric. Drake released the following statement:

"There have been questions posed to me the last few days about the writing of 'Best I Ever Had' and I figured I'd take the time to clear the air directly. I have never met Kia Shine or worked with him. I wrote the entire composition in Toronto and I borrowed one line from a Lil Wayne song that he produced the BEAT for. The claims of 25% ownership are false and for an artist to brag about splits on a song is distasteful to begin with."

On the *Billboard Hot 100* chart on July 4, 2009, Drake had two tracks in the top ten, "Best I Ever Had," and "Every Girl." This made Drake the second artist to have his first two top ten hits in the same week (the first artist was Nelly Furtado, who achieved this feat with the track, "I'm Like a Bird," and a remix of "Get Ur Freak On" with Missy Elliott).

Since releasing *So Far Gone*, Drake has enjoyed a wildly successful career, working with revered musicians such as DJ Khaled, Young Money, Jay-Z, Kanye West, Eminem, Young Jeezy, Mary J. Blige, Timbaland, Birdman, Trey Songz, and Jamie Foxx. Drake is also a talented songwriter, and has written for Alicia Keys and Dr. Dre.

Starting his Signed Career (2009–2010)

Following what *Billboard* dubbed, "one of the biggest bidding wars ever," Drake signed a recording contract with Lil Wayne's Young Money Entertainment and Universal Motown on

June 29, 2009. Before he signed, there was some speculation as to whether Drake would stay independent or if he would sign with a major label. Despite the fact that Drake signed with a major label, his management, Hip Hop Since 1978, was clear that he should continue to be viewed as an independent artist. Drake comments on signing with Young Money Entertainment:

> *"Today is a definitely a comfortable day for me, having my team now that's been in place for a couple of years. It's just a great day. It's something new, but it feels familiar...Independent is a funny term. I can go independent, but you need distribution, period. You need somebody to distribute your record and you need that army that a label has to really push the record."*

Because Drake enjoyed enormous success as an independent artist, he was able to negotiate with Universal for a remarkable contract: all publishing rights to his songs, seventy-five percent of his overall music sales revenues, and a $2 million advance. A contract this generous is virtually unheard of for a newly signed artist.

On July 31, 2009, while touring with Lil Wayne and other rap artists on the America's Most Wanted Tour, Drake fell on stage while performing "Best I Ever Had" with Lil Wayne in Camden, New Jersey. His knee was badly injured and he had to be carried off stage. On September 8, 2009, Drake underwent surgery to repair a torn anterior cruciate ligament and underwent physical therapy.

In November, 2009, Lil Wayne released a statement announcing that *Thank Me Later,* Drake's first studio album, had been completed. Originally, the album was scheduled for release in late 2009. However, the release date had to be postponed, first until March 2010, and then May 25, 2010. Ultimately, Universal Motown announced that the album would not be released until June 15, 2010.

The album featured collaborations with artists such as Kanye West, Jay-Z, and Lil Wayne. *Thank Me Later* was well received and debuted at No. 1 on the *Billboard 200*. The album has since received platinum status. Drake comments on the evolution of his music between *So Far Gone* and *Thank Me Later*:

"At the end of the day, one of the biggest things I've been toying with on 'Thank Me Later' is that it's kind of hard for me to come out and be like, 'I'm still the underdog.' I can't rap about the same things [as I did] on So Far Gone, so it's just really trying to tell the greatest story that's never been told, which is the story of a rapper's come-up, and tell it without being corny or over-bragging or sounding like, 'Feel sorry for me.' It's going to be a very interesting record because I'm really going to have to dig deep and tell stories that people can relate to. But it's kind of hard, because my life is at a very different place now."

On March 9, 2010, Drake released the first single from *Thank Me Later,* "Over." The track reached No. 14 on the *Billboard Hot 100.* Drake commented on the significance of the song.

"We took a trip to Jamaica, where I did a lot of work on my album. There was this calm before the storm, and 'Over' represented the storm to me. It's the moment. I wanted to emerge at first from this album and just let people know 'This is how I'm coming out in the public eye. I'm ready for anything.' Then, when you get the album, it's, like, 'Oh, he's still human. He's still thinking the same way.' I wanted people to understand that I could have lost it. 'Over' could have been my entire album, just 'cause that's what the industry and game will do to you if you lose yourself."

On March 12, 2010, a version of K'naan's track, "Wavin' Flag" was recorded by a collective of Canadian musicians known as the Young Artists for Haiti and released, in order to raise funds for aid after the devastating January 12, 2010, earthquake. Drake was involved in the project, and performed a solo verse near the end of the song.

"Find Your Love," the second single from *Thank Me Later*, was released on May 5, 2010. "Find Your Love" was co-produced by Kanye West and quickly became the most successful single from *Thank Me Later*, and peaked at No. 5 on the *Billboard Hot 100*. The video for "Find Your Love" tells the story of an encounter Drake has with a gang-affiliated woman (played by Malilah Michael). The video was filmed in Kingston, Jamaica, where Drake spent significant time working on his album:

"We went to Kingston, we went to this 'hood. They call it the 'gully' side. It's bad out there, real bad. They had 'Young Money' sprayed on the gates, 'Drake and Wayne,' 'cause I came to shoot the video out there. I'm talking about you drive by people's homes, they had 'Drake,' 'Young Money,' 'Drake,

Welcome Here,' 'Drake We Love You' — crazy sh--, man. It was so crazy. This dude was like, 'Original Weezy tha God! You tha boss! Weezy tha God!' It's crazy. They love us, 'cause we show love out there."

The Jamaican government was critical of the music video. Edmund Bartlett, the Minister of Tourism, felt that the video portrayed Jamaica in a negative manner and that the stereotype of a 'gun culture' was damaging to the country's image.

The third single to be released from *Thank Me Later* was, "Miss Me." This single features Lil Wayne and was released on June 1, 2010. "Miss Me" did not fare as well as "Find Your Love" and peaked at No. 15 on the *Billboard Hot 100.*

Finally, Drake's long-awaited album, *Thank Me Later,* was released on June 15, 2010. In order to promote the album, Drake was scheduled to perform a free concert with the pop group, Hanson, at South Street Seaport's Pier 17 in New York City. Concert organizers had anticipated a crowd of ten thousand people, but over twenty-five thousand fans gathered, putting the venue way over capacity. It was decided to cancel the concert due to safety concerns of overcrowding. Once the concert was cancelled, fans became angry. Several fistfights broke out and people were pushed against barricades. Several people were injured and two people were arrested. Drake felt guilty that he could not perform for his dedicated fans.

"When I was driving away, people were screaming, 'F--k Drake!' and throwing s--t at my bus. And I was frustrated because they didn't know how bad I wanted to get off that bus and perform."

The concert debacle did not harm sales, however. *Thank Me Later* sold over 447,000 copies the first week after release, the most one-week sales for any hip hop artist in 2010 (unfortunately for Drake, this record was broken by Eminem one week later). *Thank Me Later* debuted at No. 1 on the *Billboard 200.*

Also, in June 2010, it was announced that Drake would play the role of Jace Stratton in *Gears of War 3*, a much-anticipated video game. Although the Jace Stratton character only made a brief appearance in *Gears of War 2*, he is featured prominently in the *Gears of War* comic book series and is a major character in *Gears of War 3*. Drake was excited about the role:

"When Epic [Games] came to me with the role, I couldn't pass it up. They've created an amazing character in Jace, and I'm looking forward to my tour in Delta Squad."

Rod Fergusson, Epic Games executive producer, was adamant that Drake was perfect for the role of Jace Stratton:

"[Drake's EP] 'So Far Gone' had just been released, and Drake's combination of heart and grit was just what we were looking for. Rather than search for somebody who sounded like him, it was

clear that we should approach him directly ...
fortunately, he turned out to be a huge fan."

Unfortunately, the role was not meant to be. Due to a scheduling conflict, Drake was unable to perform the role of Jace Stratton.

Becoming an International Super Star (2011–Present)

On November 17, 2010, Drake announced that the title of his second studio album would be *Take Care*. Drake told the press that he was confident his second album would also be a hit.

"Don't think for a second I can't do better. For Take Care, *I'm trying to find a way to make my raps shorter but catchier. I'm trying to condense my thoughts down to sixteen bars. And it's coming out more potent."*

Although his music career was wildly successful, Drake maintained that he still wished to pursue acting:

"That's probably my biggest goal is [sic] to get back into acting and really pick the right projects. I've been reading different scripts but I know what I want to do and what type of project I want to be involved in and I've just been getting the typical projects that they'd offer to a new rapper, and it's like, ehh, that's not really what I want to do, or how I see myself...I can actually act. I've studied acting. I've studied the craft and I'm also very open to receiving a role and committing my time, whether it's two weeks, a month, two months, before the movie starts shooting to really get into that role. Like, I know what it is to do character research and really live as someone else in preparation for a movie, so that's something I'm willing to do. I care about acting a lot so I'm excited to get back into it."

In January 2011, it seemed that Drake would once again pursue his acting career. It was announced that he would be cast in the feature film, "Arbitrage," an independent film written and directed by Nicholas Jarecki. Eva Green, Richard Gere, and Susan Sarandon were also set to star in the movie. Drake's management was adamant that the actor-turned-rapper was actively involved in negotiations for the role:

"We wanna start entertaining these movie offers. Drake is looking to come out with the role no one else expects. He's not gonna be the teen heartthrob or the college kid. He wants roles where he can show his acting skills."

Unfortunately, it was later announced, in April 2011, that Drake was no longer involved in the project, as he felt it was best to fully concentrate on his next album. Drake was replaced by the actor Nate Parker. "Arbitrage" premiered at the Sundance Film Festival on January 21, 2012.

Drake's second studio album, *Take Care*, was released on November 15, 2011. The album was primarily recorded in Drake's in-home studio in Toronto. The album features guest appearances from musical superstars such as Stevie Wonder, The Weeknd, Kendrick Lamar, Lil Wayne, Nicki Minaj and Rihanna.

Despite attempts from Drake and his management to safeguard the album, it was leaked via the internet nine days before the official *Take Care* release. Drake tweeted the following message: "Listen, enjoy it, buy it if you like it...and take care until next time."

Feeling that his first studio album was rushed, Drake was more confident in *Take Care*, as he could afford to spend the extra time to hone his craft:

"To be 100 percent honest ... I wasn't necessarily happy with Thank Me Later. People loved it [but] I just knew what I was capable of with a little more time. I'm very confident in Take Care. I definitely

made the exact album that I wanted. Will it appear that way to the world? I'm not sure, because it's definitely different. It's not 15 'I'm On Ones.' It's not 'She Will.' I'm very happy with this album. More so than I've ever been with a project."

Take Care was originally slated for release on October 24, 2011 (Drake's birthday), but had to be postponed in order to obtain clearance for three samples used on the album. Drake released the following statement on his website:

"I have completed 19 songs (17 on physical and 2 on bonus), and have run into a roadblock of clearing 3 samples in time to make the October 24th date. My options were to take the songs off and make the birthday release happen, or to take an extra couple weeks to get the paperwork right and give you the album the way I NEED you to hear it. The choice was clear as day for me. November 15th you will get Take Care the exact way I created it

with no trimmings. This music means too much to me to get attached to dates and I do apologize for the delay but I promise that it is only for the benefit of our experience together."

In order to promote the new album before the official release, Drake made the track, "Marvin's Room" available for download on his website on June 9, 2011, and on iTunes on July 22, 2011. The corresponding music video was released on June 28, 2011. The song was not initially intended for inclusion on *Take Care*, but, due to the overwhelming success, it was put on the album.

Unfortunately not all of the press about "Marvin's Room" was positive. The track opens with a midnight "drunk dial" from a female friend. Recently, Drake's ex-girlfriend, Ericka Lee, filed a suit against Drake claiming that, as she provided the voice on the other end of the telephone call in the track, she is entitled to co-writer royalties. Ericka Lee claimed that she had both a business and personal relationship with Drake that started in early 2010 and ended mid-2011. Supposedly the two would routinely exchange poems and lyrics and discussed collaborating on a musical project. According to her lawsuit, it was originally planned that Lee would perform a hook for "Marvin's Room," as well as a monologue to frame the lyrics.

Drake denies Lee's claim and has an entirely different account of how he was inspired to write "Marvin's Room." According to Drake, he was in the recording studio with producer Noah '40' Shebib when he received the phone call that would later be used in the track:

"Middle of recording I got a call from this girl, and she had been drinking. Because I was recording, I just put the phone on the speaker and sat it on the music stand. [Noah] '40' thought so quick to record it. I went back to recording more melodies. As I was recording, he was taking pieces of the conversation out ... You know where the story is going. At the

end of the night we had a song called 'Marvin's Room.'"

In order to settle the lawsuit out of court, Drake offered Erika Lee two percent of the publishing royalties. When she refused, he raised the offer to five percent, as well as a $50,000 settlement. Lee once again refused and is seeking co-writing credit as well as damages.

On February 4, 2012, a spokesperson for Drake released the following statement:

"This claim is entirely without merit and our client has not engaged in any wrongful conduct. Ericka Lee consented to the use of her voice in the song 'Marvin's Room' prior to its release. Lee asked only for the credit she received as 'Syren Lyric Muse,' and she did not ask for any compensation. It was only after she retained a lawyer that there was a demand for payment. Drake tried for months to

resolve the matter amicably, and he now looks forward to being vindicated in court."

The first official single to be released from *Take Care* was the song, "Headlines," which peaked at No. 13 on the *Billboard Hot 100*, making "Headlines" his second-highest debut. The song was first made available on Drake's website on July 31, 2011, and was released to American radio on August 9, 2011.

"Headlines" reached platinum status in Canada on November 17, 2011, after selling forty thousand copies. Platinum status in the United States was reached on February 7, 2012 after selling a million copies. Drake even had the honor of performing "Headlines" on the ice at the 2012 National Hockey League (NHL) All-Star Game in Kanata, Ontario.

Although Drake felt that "Headlines" was not the strongest track on *Take Care*, he chose to release it first as he felt it carried an important message:

"By no means is it the best song on my album, it really is just the song for this moment right now. I always try to put forth a song with a message. A lot of people pick their single by what's the strongest song. I don't really do that. I like to make sure that the content is really relevant for right now... Since I've been gone for a minute, trying to craft this album, a lot of it came out in that song. And just reassuring people, reassuring the fans, this is really in my opinion my best project."

The second single from *Take Care* was "Make Me Proud," featuring fellow musician Nicki Minaj. The song was available for download on October 16, 2011, and released to American radio on October 25, 2011. "Make Me Proud" did not have a stellar debut, starting at No. 97 on the *Billboard Hot 100*, but soon jumped to No. 9 in its second week.

As "Make Me Proud" is about Drake's ideal woman, it is no coincidence that Nicki Minaj is featured:

"If there's any woman in my life that's the ideal woman for me, it's definitely Nicki. I like the stripped-down Nicki. I like Nicki with no makeup, black hair, some casual clothes in a recording booth rapping an amazing verse. That's sexy to me. I know some great women, but all jokes aside, Nicki is somebody I could spend my life with because I think we understand each other."

The third single to be released from *Take Care* was the song, "The Motto." This song was a bonus track on *Take Care* and features Lil Wayne. It was released on American radio on November 29, 2011, after being released on Drake's website on November 1, 2011. "The Motto" debuted at No. 18 on the *Billboard Hot 100*, and reached platinum status once sales exceeded one million copies.

The fourth and most recent single is the title track, "Take Care," featuring the singing superstar, Rihanna. The song was released on urban radio on February 14, 2010, and mainstream American radio on February 21, 2012. "Take Care" debuted at No. 9 on the *Billboard Hot 100*. "Take Care" marks the second time that Drake has collaborated with Rihanna, as he is featured in the single, "What's My Name?" on her fifth album, *Loud*. The music video for "Take Care" was filmed in February, 2012, and was directed by Yoann Lemoine.

Drake was slated to work on a joint album with Lil Wayne, however, on November 4, 2011, it was announced that this project would be postponed indefinitely, as Jay-Z and Kanye West had recently released a joint album entitled, *Watch the Throne*. Lil Wayne and Drake felt that their joint album would be compared to *Watch the Throne*:

> *"Me and Wayne scrapped the idea of a collaboration album. We just agreed that it would be looked upon as... It would be sort of this competition [with* Watch the Throne*]. I feel like it would get caught in this whirlwind of hype."*

Unfortunately another collaborative project of Drake's was recently shelved. Drake was working with Rick Ross on a duet mixtape entitled, "Y.O.L.O.," "You Only Live Once," Drake's motto for life. However, the mixtape was put on hold when Rick Ross began suffering health problems:

"I have been working on a mixtape with Ross...A mixtape called Y.O.L.O. [That means] 'You Only Live Once.' I've been working on that for the last couple of weeks. We haven't really connected because he's been going through this thing with his health. I've been stashing my little beats and verses."

On October 14, 2011, at the age of 35, Ross suffered a seizure while on board a flight en route to a concert in Memphis, Tennessee. The aircraft made an emergency landing and Ross was taken to a hospital for treatment. Later that day, he posted on Twitter that he was being discharged from the hospital and would be performing the scheduled concert in Memphis that same night. However, after boarding a private jet, Ross suffered yet another seizure. He was once again taken to a hospital where he was stabilized.

Personal Life

Named "2010 Man of the Year" by *GQ* Magazine, Drake is a silent partner in an upscale Italian restaurant in New York City and owns a bachelor pad in Miami.

Drake has the privilege of calling many famous people his friend, even former President, Bill Clinton. Drake met Clinton when he was invited to perform a concert for a Clinton Foundation fundraiser in March 2011. The experience left a distinct impression on Drake:

> *"One of my favorite pictures I have in my house is of me and Bill [Clinton] and I'm wearing a zebra Supreme jacket and he's wearing a suit. It's wild!"*

Not content with meeting a former US President, Drake has also been trying to meet the current President, President Barack

Obama. However, he has encountered some difficulty due to his status as a Canadian citizen:

> *"I ran into somebody who works for Barack Obama the other day, and she's like, 'I'm so sorry we haven't called you, but we can't have Canadian citizens perform or be a part of U.S. politics.' ... I was like, 'Well, I'm a dual citizen!' And she was like, 'No way! Well, you've got to come now.' So I think I might actually get a chance to meet Barack."*

Politics aside, Drake is also an avid sports fan. He favors the men's college basketball team, the Kentucky Wildcats, and is reportedly good friends with head coach, John Calipari. He has even made public appearances at games, such as on January 2, 2009, when he attended the game against the University of Louisville, and on October 16, 2009, when he attended the "Big Blue Madness" event. He also performed a concert for fans at the University of Kentucky on April 27, 2010.

Romantic Relationships

Drake has been involved in several high-profile romantic relationships, one of which is with Keshia Chanté, a fellow Canadian singer. Drake's song "Deceiving" refers to his relationship with Chanté, and his relationship with her mother, Tessa, in the second verse:

"When I say I'm serious, you claim you're only teasing...What up, Tessa? I love you like my own mama, and your daughter's getting grown, mama, and me, I'm just here working, waiting, patient for her to be ready for love and leave alone drama."

In a May 2009 interview, Drake addressed speculation on his former relationship with Chanté:

"Would I call Keshia Chante an ex? I'd be proud to say she is an ex. I'm proud to say we had our time, when we were, like, 16 years old. She's great. She's one of the first people in the industry that I met, we just connected."

Later in 2009, Drake did two separate remixes of Chanté's song, "Fallen," in which he addresses their past relationship. In the first version, Drake raps, "Keshia, Keshia, do you remember the old us? They said we'd never be together, that's what they told us. Immature kids, to entrepreneur kids." In the second remix he says, "You just hold it down for your boy until the plaques arrive, that's why I love you."

Also in 2009, Drake had a brief relationship with international superstar Rihanna, referred to in his song, "Fireworks." Drake dated Rihanna following the incident with Chris Brown in which Brown physically abused Rihanna, Brown's girlfriend at the time.

Drake never thought he would be dating a pop icon such as Rihanna and the relationship took him by surprise:

"I came straight from Toronto, just a kid that was trying to get out of my mom's house, and the first person I meet is a girl that's the biggest person you could possibly meet at my age. So I meet her and it was just mind-blowing. I couldn't believe she'd even want to talk to me."

There was a rumor that circulated in the media stating that Brown retaliated against Drake for dating Rihanna. The rumor was started by DJ Whoo Kid who stated in an interview:

"I think [Drake] got elbowed by Chris Brown, too, but that never came out. In the chin, like in the corner. Left part. Man down. Simple as that."

Drake maintained that the rumor was false:

"I respect Chris Brown. I'd like to call myself a friend—I don't know if I'm allowed to do that. But I definitely didn't get elbowed in my face. Somebody would've got knocked the f--k out."

Later, DJ Whoo Kid stated on his Twitter account that the entire story had been a joke.

There have also been rumors that Drake has had a relationship with Nicki Minaj. The two had a 'fake' Twitter marriage and have collaborated together on various projects. Minaj, a fellow Young Money hip hop star, met Drake when they were on tour together:

"Me and Nicki have a really playful relationship. When I was on tour ... I saw Nicki for the first time and, like, literally fell in love. She had this snap-back hat on that said 'Minaj.' She used to wear that every single day. She was like a theater student and she was so cold at rapping."

Minaj denies that the two have ever been more than just friends. However, Drake is adamant that he has genuine feelings for her.

"I've always really, actually, really had a crush on her, always really loved her, and she's always just looked at me as, like, her little brother."